THE BOOK OF THE

A4 PACIFICS

Photographic Accompaniment No.3

By Peter Coster

In June 1947 the die was cast and the LNER had just six months left in existence. ANDREW K. McCOSH is in Doncaster Paint Shop being restored to garter blue livery, the right and proper livery for an A4 (in my view). The Doncaster painters usually rendered the Cross symbol of Kings Cross as a Maltese cross, typical of the pride in their workmanship. A freshly painted Pacific was a joy to behold.

IRWELL PRESS Ltd.

ISBN 1-903266-66-1
ISBN 978-1-903266-66-3

First published in the United Kingdom in 2006
by Irwell Press Limited, 59A, High Street, Clophill,
Bedfordshire MK45 4BE
Printed by Newnorth Print, Bedford

INTRODUCTION

This is our third collection of photographs of the 35 A4 Pacifics and the W1 4-6-2-2. With *The Book of the A4 Pacifics* and the previous two *Accompaniments*, a considerable portfolio has been built up. Of course it is not quite as we would have wished, for (as ever) there are too few of pre-war days and rather more of their latter days, which gives a false impression to those not lucky enough to see the engines in their prime. We would have liked to include the work of famous names such as Cyril Herbert, who specialised in the pre-war LNER and the Bishop of Railway Photography, Eric Treacy, to name but two and perhaps this might be possible in a future *Accompaniment*.

A lot of photographs were taken on shed, which cramps one's style when trying to depict the engines working hard, or at speed. It is easy to forget how slow emulsions were half a century ago, and how expensive good cameras with large apertures were. Not every day was sunny and not many engines were clean, taxing the ingenuity of the photographer and his light meter, and often calling for a longer exposure than was practicable just in order to get a decent shot of an elusive engine.

BASIC A4 NAMES AND NUMBERS.
There are potentially four different numbers for any A4 and the namings were complicated by renaming and even recycling in the case of WOODCOCK...

Loco	First No.	Original Name
60001 SIR RONALD MATTHEWS	4500	*GARGANEY*
60002 SIR MURROUGH WILSON	4499	*POCHARD*
60003 ANDREW K. McCOSH	4494	*OSPREY*
60004 WILLIAM WHITELAW	4462	*GREAT SNIPE*
60005 SIR CHARLES NEWTON	4901	*CAPERCAILLIE*
60006 SIR RALPH WEDGWOOD	4466	*HERRING GULL*
60007 SIR NIGEL GRESLEY	4498	-
60008 DWIGHT D. EISENHOWER	4496	*GOLDEN SHUTTLE*
60009 UNION OF SOUTH AFRICA	4488	-
60010 DOMINION OF CANADA	4489	*WOODCOCK*
60011 EMPIRE OF INDIA	4490	-
60012 COMMONWEALTH OF AUSTRALIA	4491	-
60013 DOMINION OF NEW ZEALAND	4492	-
60014 SILVER LINK	2509	-
60015 QUICKSILVER	2510	-
60016 SILVER KING	2511	-
60017 SILVER FOX	2512	-
60018 SPARROW HAWK	4463	-
60019 BITTERN	4464	-
60020 GUILLEMOT	4465	-
60021 WILD SWAN	4467	-
60022 MALLARD	4468	-
60023 GOLDEN EAGLE	4482	-
60024 KINGFISHER	4483	-
60025 FALCON	4484	-
60026 MILES BEEVOR	4485	*KESTREL*
60027 MERLIN	4486	-
60028 WALTER K. WHIGHAM	4487	*SEA EAGLE*
60029 WOODCOCK	4493	-
60030 GOLDEN FLEECE	4495	*GREAT SNIPE*
60031 GOLDEN PLOVER	4497	-
60032 GANNET	4900	-
60033 SEAGULL	4902	-
60034 LORD FARINGDON	4903	*PEREGRINE*
4469 SIR RALPH WEDGWOOD	4469	*GADWALL**

There were two number series given to the A4s in 1946. The first, 580-613 appeared only on three or four before the 1-34 sequence was arrived at. It was the addition of 60,000 to these after nationalisation that gave the familiar BR numbers.
***Destroyed in Second World War air raid on York.**

In a beautifully composed picture, the up 'Flying Scotsman' crosses the Royal Border Bridge behind an unidentified A4, possibly one of the Nos.4493-4498 engines.

SIR RONALD MATTHEWS at Langley troughs in June 1962 with an up Newcastle express. By this time the Gateshead A4s, with their double chimneys, were a more common sight in the south. Tender non-corridor No.5674. (P J Coster)

SIR RONALD MATTHEWS at the head of a down express passing Darlington in May 1947. The train looks as though it might be the 'Flying Scotsman' to judge from the quality of the stock. The A4 has the metal relief letters and numbers, and is fairly clean for a Gateshead resident. The tender is A4 non-corridor No.5674.

SIR MURROUGH WILSON at speed with a down express at Cadwell, latish in the day by the look of the shadows. The date must fall between July 1957 and March 1959 and the tender is the A4 non-corridor No.5673, retained throughout. (A Scarsbrook, Initial Photographics)

SIR MURROUGH WILSON in New England repair shops, temporarily reduced to 0-6-2 status while the bogie axleboxes are repaired. The date must be 1958-61, before the ubiquitous electrification notices were applied. One wonders at the weight distribution of the locomotive with the bogie removed and the front unsupported. The leading and second coupled axles now have an additional 20 tons imposed, which is hardly an insignificant excess. I hope the boiler was emptied beforehand, which would reduce the load on the coupled wheels by a similar amount. It is to be hoped that substantial members of the fitting staff are working in the firebox and cab lest the engine tip forward. What might appear as a supporting jack is in fact a headlamp hanging on the cylinder drain. (B Richardson, The Transport Treasury)

No.4494, in LNER apple green livery, with her original name OSPREY. That name gave way to the prosaic ANDREW K McCOSH near the end of 1942. No. 4494 went new to Heaton, an odd choice one might think, but then she moved to Doncaster and then Grantham before her first overhaul and change to garter blue livery. The express may have been the second portion of the down 'Flying Scotsman', which Heaton worked on certain weekdays, but there is no information to indicate whether it is a down (probably) or up train. If the A4 was at Heaton, as I think it is, the date must be late summer 1937, but 1938 if not. Nor is there any identification of the troughs, which might be Langley, Werrington or Wiske Moor, all of which had four tracks. The signal is not GNR, and although it may be LNER upper quadrant, I would opt for Wiske Moor.

ANDREW K McCOSH, just a week out Doncaster Works in garter blue, with its BR number, backing out of Kings Cross Station to Top Shed on March 9th 1949. From its position, it looks as though the A4 has arrived in the suburban station, perhaps from Cambridge, on a running-in turn. Tender: original A4 corridor No.5649. (B K B Green, Initial Photographics)

ANDREW K McCOSH, as LNER No.3, in garter blue livery, heading an up express past Greenwood signalbox. The up bracket is still carrying somersault signals, and Hadley Wood South Tunnel has that perpetual smoky haze from the engines of down trains pulling hard against the gradient. Period: June 1947-48. Tender: original A4 corridor No.5649. (Ted's Dad)

ANDREW K McCOSH is racing through Hadley Wood on July 4th 1953, running early, with the 12 noon from Newcastle. At the time it was the balancing turn with the previous day's 'Tees-Tyne Pullman', which is the reversed headboard on the A4. It was a reasonably fast train, if for no other reason than the crew would have had their top link brethren breathing down their necks with the up 'Flying Scotsman' just behind. On this day it was SIR NIGEL GRESLEY following a block behind, and neither of her crews were known to loiter! The engine has the A4 non-corridor tender No.5642, originally on MALLARD. Considering the A4 has come from Newcastle, she has plenty of coal left. (B K B Green, Initial Photographics)

The 17.15 Glasgow pulls out of Waverley behind WILLIAM WHITELAW, as seen from The Mound Tunnel, on June 8th 1958; the tender is the former W1 A3 type corridor No.5484. (The Transport Treasury)

WILLIAM WHITELAW stands at St. Margarets on May 15th 1965. This was another shed where a clean engine was a passing novelty, although WILLIAM was a visitor from Ferryhill, in good external condition for 1965. The tender is the A3 corridor built for the W1, No.5484. (A Scarsbrook, Initial Photographics)

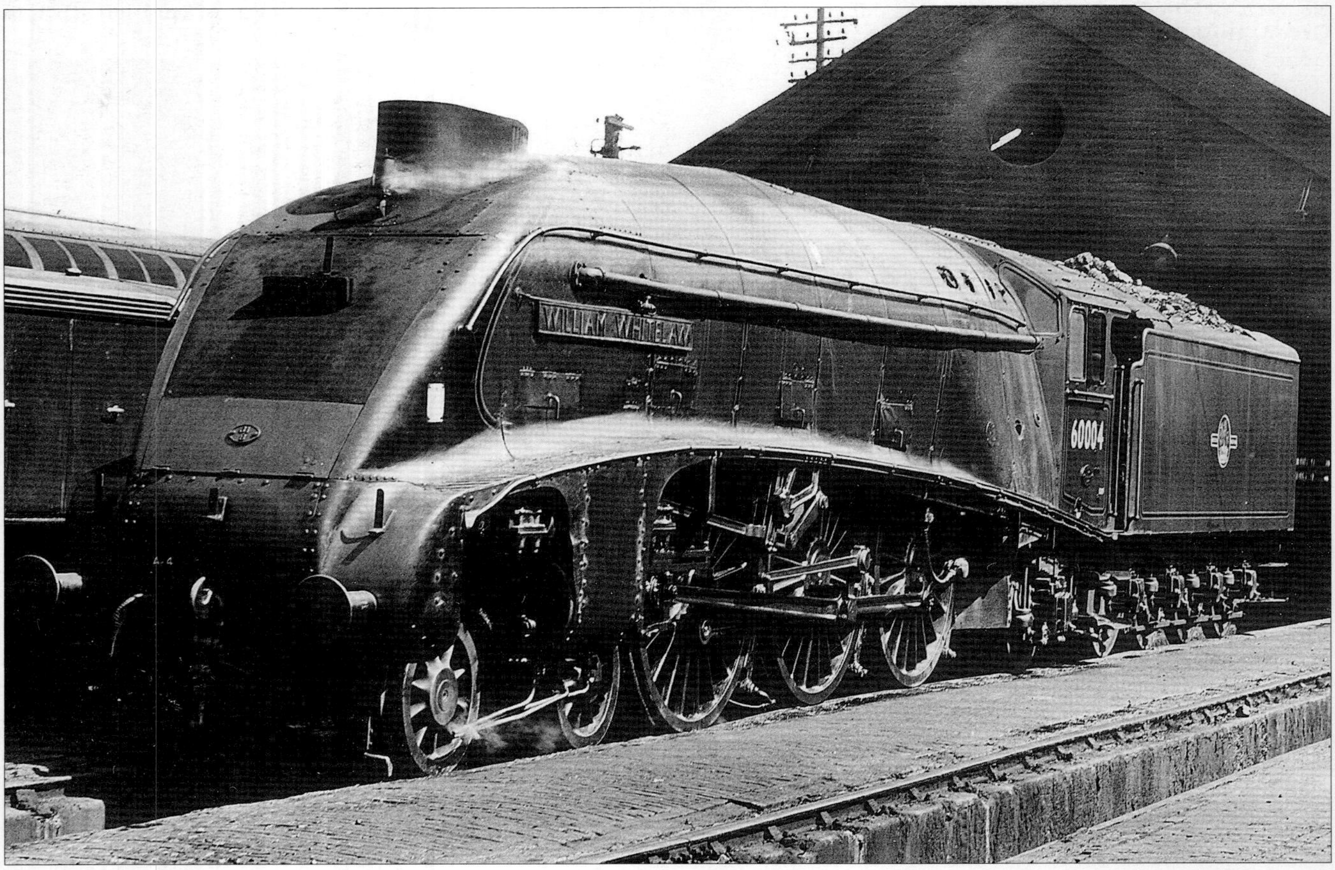

SIR CHARLES NEWTON in BR dark blue livery, between late 1949 and early 1951. She looks to be coming off shed, but it could be almost any of the principal main line depots. The sunlight is low, behind the camera, which suggests Doncaster or York.

SIR RALPH WEDGWOOD, running light engine near Arbroath. Ferryhill cleaners clearly had short arms! The date is May 21st 1965, and the A4 has A4 non-corridor tender No.5675. (A R Scarsbrook, Initial Photographics)

SIR NIGEL GRESLEY at York shed, in BR blue on July 1st 1951. The tender is A3 corridor tender No.5324. (B K B Green, Initial Photographics)

SIR NIGEL GRESLEY on the up 'Flying Scotsman' at milepost 7, north of New Southgate. I think the train is the 1928 stock, which means that it is summer 1938, as the new stock did not enter service until the autumn. The tender is No.5329. The down main signals are Southgate's advance starter and Cemetery's distant. They were replaced later but were still mounted on a tall post so as to be sighted above the dark background of Oakleigh Road bridge and Barnet Tunnel.

SIR NIGEL GRESLEY at speed with a down express. The year is 1958 but the location is not stated. I would hazard a guess that it is north of Grantham, above (or possibly below) Peascliffe, but no more precise than that. The tender is A3 corridor tender No.5324. (A H Lucas, The Transport Treasury)

SIR NIGEL GRESLEY on a down express at New Southgate in August 1961. Tender No.5324. The bricked in archway in the intimidatingly high wall of the Colney Hatch County Asylum was once the siding entrance for the establishment's coal supplies, accessed from a wagon turntable on the down siding. (Canon Brian C. Bailey)

In the days of through working and frequent failures up to September 1951, DWIGHT D EISENHOWER is at Escrick with the down 'Northumbrian', on July 27th 1950; the A4 has her original A4 corridor tender No.5651. (Cawston Bequest, Canon Brian C. Bailey Collection)

An unusual photograph, taken at Grantham. One might wonder why, but a detailed knowledge of the GN would lead to that conclusion. The down 'Flying Scotsman' in October 1956 was worked by New England as far as Grantham, and an A1 thereon to Newcastle. A Kings Cross A4 such as DWIGHT D EISENHOWER would be involved only as a replacement. All engine changing for northbound trains involved movements at the north end and not the south. Brian Bailey has reminded me that if the A4 had worked the 10.40 from Kings Cross she may have reversed her empty train into the south sidings. The A4 would then run forward, on to the down main if the down slow was occupied by a stopping service. As the A4 would later return south with the 'Scotsman', perhaps the fireman has put the headboard in position already. On closer study the driver appears to be Alf Gymer of Kings Cross which supports this theory. Otherwise with mechanical signalling one only needed an obstinate facing point lock to throw operations into confusion. The engine has her original tender, A4 corridor No.5651. (The Transport Treasury)

An official photograph of LNER No.4496 in September 1945 after renaming. The tender is A4 corridor No.5651.

UNION OF SOUTH AFRICA stands at the end of Kings Cross platform 6 waiting for the signal to move to the Station Loco yard for coaling. She is in BR blue livery, and has worked the 'Capitals Limited' up from Edinburgh. The condition of the paintwork would suggest that it is 1951. The A4 has its painted coat of arms in place, together with the Flaman drive. The springbok plaque was fitted later, on the driver's side only. The tender is the A4 corridor removed from SILVER KING, No.5591. (The Transport Treasury)

A line-up at Haymarket in August 1961. UNION OF SOUTH AFRICA is joined by a filthy BROWN JACK and a named B1 4-6-0, MURRAY OF ELIBANK. Haymarket had a number of English Electric type 4s, one of which is on the extreme right. (J Robertson, The Transport Treasury)

Contemporary publicity shot of DOMINION OF CANADA at Kings Cross, possibly taken soon after the CPR bell was mounted.

DOMINION OF CANADA, just out of Doncaster Works after conversion to double blast and losing the bell in the process. She is on the 7.35 from Nottingham, the 'Mark Lane Flyer', approaching New Southgate, in January 1958. A3 corridor tender No.5328. (P J Coster)

Now a double Kylchap engine, a superbly clean DOMINION OF CANADA races through Ganwick with the 'Flying Scotsman'. She will run through to Newcastle on this duty. The date is September 9th 1959, and the tender is A3 corridor No.5328.

DOMINION OF CANADA arrives at platform 8 at Kings Cross with the 7.50 from Leeds, July 14th 1952; the tender is A3 corridor No.5328. (B K B Green, Initial Photographics)

The Flying Scotsman breasts Stoke Summit in fine style, with DOMINION OF CANADA's driver ringing the bell, something which is unusual in a photograph. I think it is the 1938 set, which places the date between late 1938 and September 1939. An O2 with the GN cab waits for the road on the down goods. Tender is A3 corridor No.5326. (Cawston Bequest, Canon Brian C Bailey Collection)

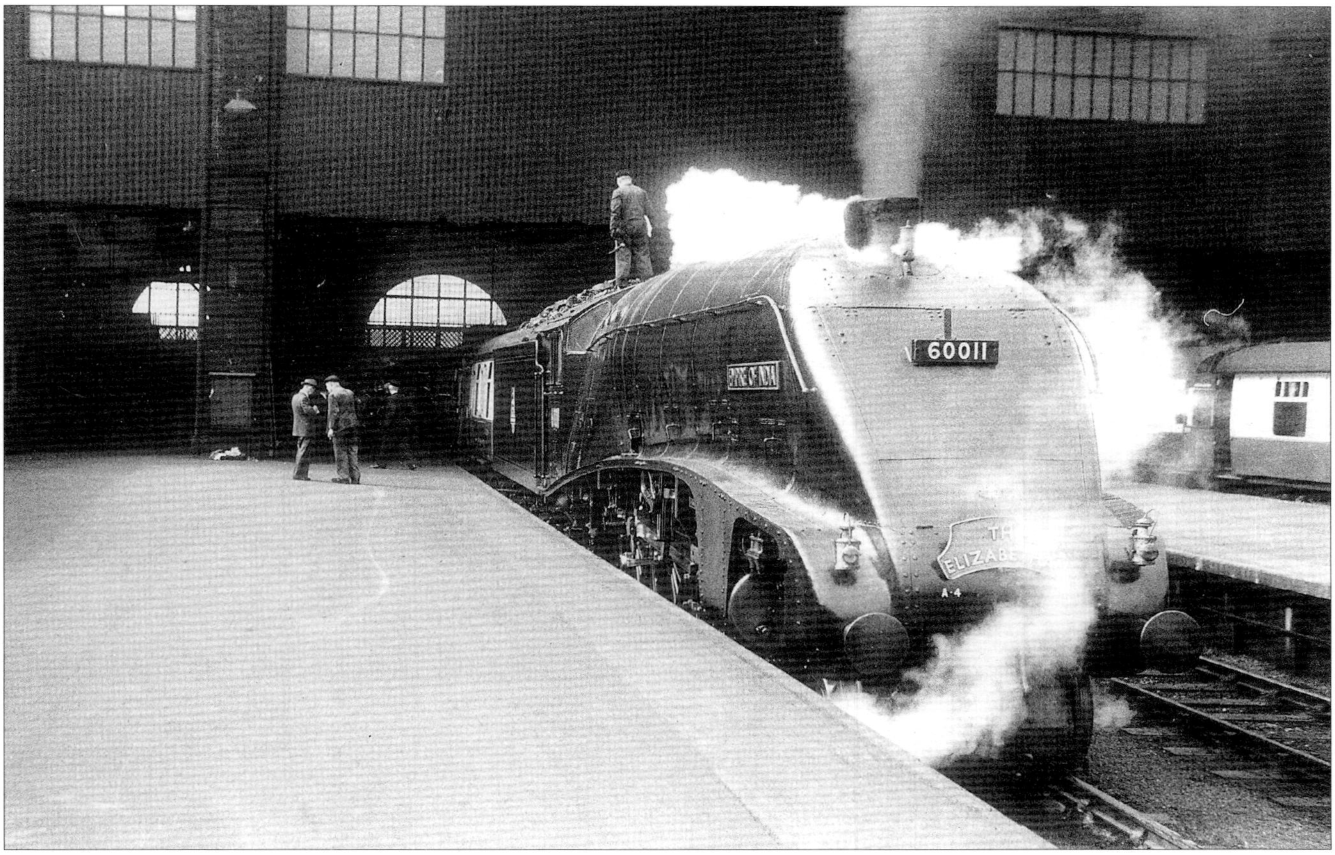

EMPIRE OF INDIA of Haymarket reversed on to the 'Elizabethan' at Kings Cross, during the 1955 season. Driver Fred Deeley is talking to a locomotive inspector, while his athletic fireman surveys the contents of the tender from above, coal pick in hand. A good enough justification for the later introduction of electrification 'flashes', fixed where staff might encroach on the mandatory 6ft clearance from live equipment. The A4 had an A3 corridor tender, in this case No.5326. (P J Coster)

EMPIRE OF INDIA, now a Ferryhill engine, at St. Rollox shed, about 1963. Tender: A3 corridor No.5328. (A Scarsbrook, Initial Photographics)

Above. Now converted to double blast, with AWS, a Western Australian Railway chime whistle, and viewed from the fireman's side we can see, remarkably, the Flaman drive bracket. Having ridden on this A4 I am fairly sure that no recorder was present, and the lack of any drive shafts would confirm this. COMMONWEALTH OF AUSTRALIA is looking somewhat travel-stained, and the date must be well after mid-1960. A4 corridor tender No.5646. (The Transport Treasury)

Below. COMMONWEALTH OF AUSTRALIA pounds up the last few yards of the sharp rise from Craigentinny through Calton Tunnel into Waverley station with an express from Kings Cross. I would guess that the train is the second part of the 'Flying Scotsman', the 10.5 departure, No.52 down, which will continue to Glasgow Queen Street. It looks as though Waverley East was not ready for 52 down and the A4 has been checked around St. Margarets. The rarely illustrated Waverley Goods Depot is beyond the A4. The period is July 1954, and the tender is the A4 corridor No.5646 which she always had. Random Thought: I recall a trip in 1956 with this engine on the Non-stop. We were going well, Ted Hailstone following his usual practice of running hard to get time back after no less than three signals slow to clear. I timed her touching 100 briefly at Arlesey and then, after the rise to Langford, 98 after Biggleswade. As we passed an overhanging tree obscuring the driver's vision, there was the Sandy distant – on! I was standing behind the driver and saw it as well. Ted dropped the brake on hard but it seemed to make little difference. I was advised in peremptory tones to make myself scarce, as a Scottish Region loco inspector was in the train. Looking out of the leading brake composite as we shuddered to a halt, with the loco and tender past the home signal, I could see the light WD beyond the station regaining the down slow. Too close for comfort! What possessed the signalman to let the WD go through the bottleneck with the Non-stop all but on the block I cannot say. Moreover, with the level crossings beyond at Everton and Tempsford he would have been given 'train on line' early. No doubt he had three days unpaid leave in which to reflect on the error of his ways. (J Robertson, The Transport Treasury)

In the summer of 1960 COMMONWEALTH OF AUSTRALIA stands at the head of a number of engines awaiting attention at Doncaster, shedmate HORNET'S BEAUTY standing behind. The A4 is in steam, but the rest appear dead. The A4 has returned to the Plant for casual repairs. It is still carrying a normal A4 chime whistle; shortly afterwards a larger Western Australia Railways chime was fitted at Haymarket shed. Tender: A4 corridor No.5646. (D H Beecroft, The Transport Treasury)

DOMINION OF NEW ZEALAND hard at work with the up 'Flying Scotsman' near Retford, probably on the climb south towards Markham, August 7th 1956. The ganger clearly takes a pride in his section, and one can still see the stone edging to the down line that was popular at a time when we had adequate manpower for such things. Tender: Hoffman A4 corridor No.5647. (B K B Green, Initial Photographics)

DOMINION OF NEW ZEALAND at Waverley station, waiting the Right Away with the up 'Flying Scotsman' in 1938. Her tender No.5647 has been provided with Hoffman roller bearings, but the BG behind the engine looks like the 1938 brake that entered service in autumn of that year. The resignalling of Waverley with colour lights seems to be under way with the point motor by the cab, and the shunt signal not yet in use. (K J MacDonald, The Transport Treasury)

SILVER LINK and GOLDEN FLEECE at Kings Cross shed. No other information is given, but the date must be between May 1954 and October 1957 as defined by the loss of long guard irons and fitting of double Kylchaps. It has the feel of midday in winter. GOLDEN FLEECE has the valancing removed behind the left-hand cylinder. (The Transport Treasury)

The north portal of Hadley Wood South Tunnel and the adjacent old station at Hadley Wood were always wreathed in smoke from down trains, as the draught seemed to carry the exhaust northwards. As a result the station had a wonderful atmosphere and a 'perfume' of hard working steam engines – and firemen. SILVER LINK, in pre-Hailstone days, bursts through the billowing clouds with a down express. The year is 1950 but by May she had moved to Kings Cross, while in August she was fitted with ATC equipment. The tender is the Timken A4 corridor No.5590. (Cawston Bequest, Canon Brian C. Bailey Collection)

Only the engine number is given here, but I think that this in fact was a special occasion. I believe it is the second VIP special for the Royal Wedding on June 8th 1961. QUICKSILVER, in immaculate condition, was the second A4 to emerge from Top Shed, and the running numbers of the two trains were 500 and 501. The location is strange, for the East Coast tracks are paired by direction and not speed as is the case farther to the west. Therefore it must be at some point approaching York north of Chaloners Whin, with the lines from south-west Yorkshire on the right. The tender is A4 corridor No.5589. (The Transport Treasury)

QUICKSILVER races south through Newark with an up Newcastle express in August 1960. Tender: A4 corridor No.5589. (D H Beecroft, The Transport Treasury)

QUICKSILVER, after its first repair with number on the front and extended front drawbar and buffers. (R J Buckley, Initial Photographics)

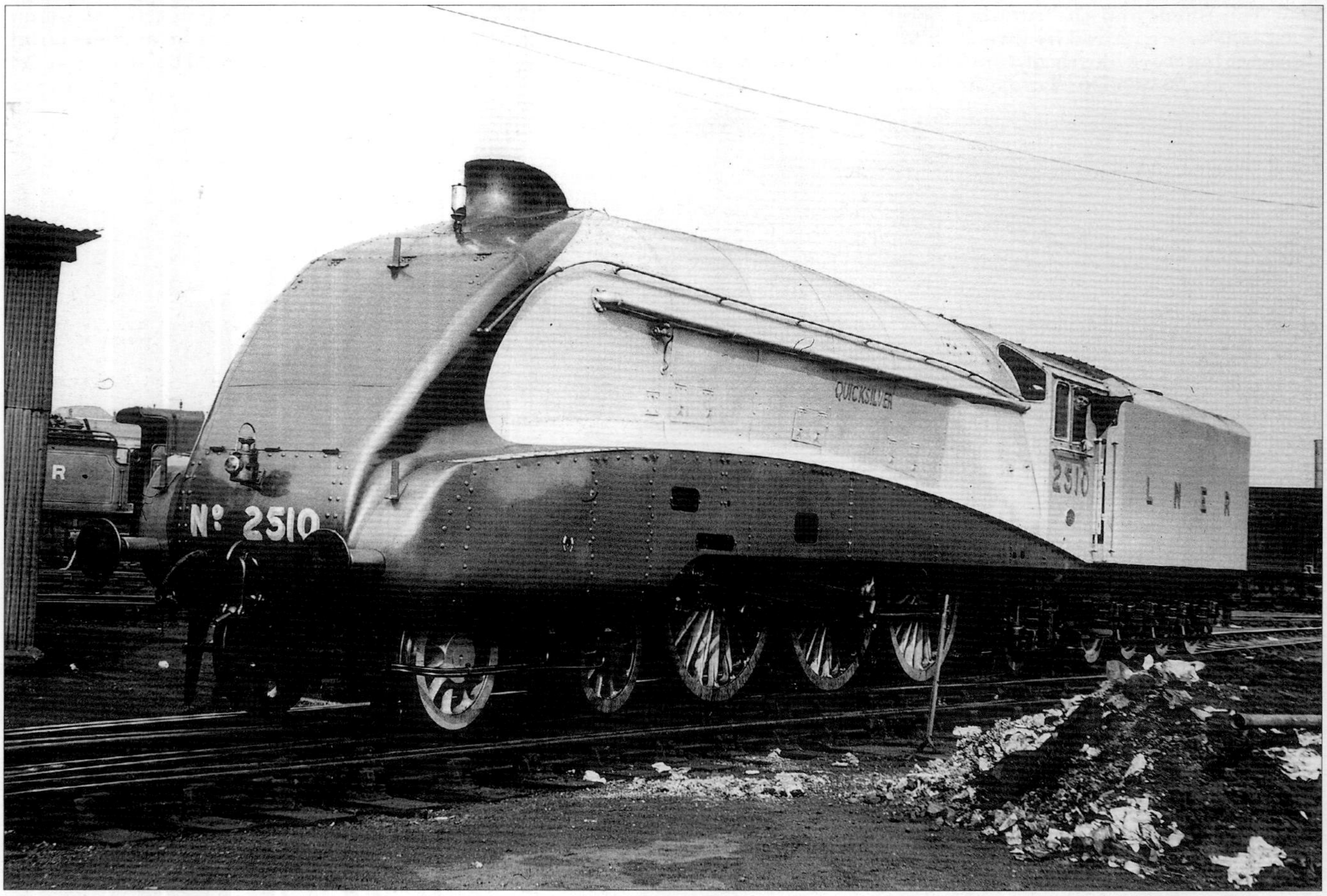

Clearly we are not looking at an A4 from London or Edinburgh! A filthy SILVER KING starts the descent of Cockburnspath Bank with the 6.48 York-Edinburgh, which seems to comprise largely of baggage vans, on June 2nd 1961. The tender is non-corridor No.5636. (J F Aylard)

From September 1951 until the autumn of 1952 the 16.05 York Dringhouses fast fitted freight was usually worked by a Gateshead Pacific. On August 12th 1952 SILVER KING runs slowly through New Southgate on the down slow. (Canon Brian C. Bailey)

Above. On the route long since closed, from Bridge of Dun to Perth, easier gradients are encountered but at Forfar curvature rivalled the East Coast main line stations. Although most trains were lightweight by comparison with the 1950s, the 15.30 required a heavier hand on the regulator. SILVER KING gets her big train under way from Forfar on July 4th 1964. Tender: A4 non-corridor No.5636. (M Mensing)

Below. A well-known shot of SILVER KING bursting from one of the Hadley Wood tunnels into the old station with the 'Flying Scotsman', going hard. The direction is not stated, but Willie Yeadon, in publishing the shot in his A4 Register, took it to be the up train. With respect I beg to differ. The cable route ran on the up side, just visible in the clouds of exhaust steam. The headshunt of the old goods yard is not in camera, and the signal seems more likely to be the up platform starter: there would not be one on the down so close to the goods yard turnout, and there is no advance colour light signal. Both Crescent Road over the South Tunnel and Waggon Road over the North would look very rural in 1938-39. And the lighting of the A4 says 'down' to me. The volcanic exhaust is quite something, suggesting a rather more heroic assault on the 'Northern Heights' than we were used to post-war. The up platform starter is of course one of the GNR's magnificent somersault signals, and what appear to be a warning bell nearby, probably to warn platform staff of the approach of an (fast) up train. This is the period of the winter service, 1938-1939. The conventional wisdom is that white lining of platforms started in wartime, which would appear to be at variance with the picture. The tender is A4 corridor No.5591. (Gresley Society Trust, I McCabe Collection)

SILVER KING in filthy condition heads a down express beyond Golf Club Bridge at Knebworth on June 24th 1961. Either the tender is overloaded or the slipstream has caught the loose rubber cab sheeting. The tender is A4 non-corridor No.5636. (G W Goslin, Gresley Society Trust)

SILVER FOX brings an up express through Harringay amid a forest of somersault signals in its first weeks of service, 1935. (The Transport Treasury)

The A4s looked magnificent when clean, but when filthy, like Stanier's streamlined Pacifics they looked awful. In spring 1947, a dirty SILVER FOX reaches the top of the climb out of London at Potters Bar with a train of motley coaches; one suspects that are in much the same state as the locomotive! The tender is the original No.5592. (Cawston Bequest, Canon Brian C. Bailey Collection)

On April 22nd 1948 after a general overhaul, SILVER FOX roars northwards with the 'Yorkshire Pullman'. It is a well-known photograph, but it is one of Arthur Cawston's finest. Childhood memories include the famous down main somersault signal, which clanked unmistakably when a down express was signalled, inviting conjecture as to what was to come. Tender No.5592. (Cawston Bequest, Canon Brian C. Bailey Collection)

The second up 'Capitals Limited' of the season races over the last miles through Greenwood into London seven minutes early on July 1st 1952 behind SILVER FOX. The tender is No.5592. (Cawston Bequest, Canon Brian C. Bailey Collection)

SILVER FOX, in superb condition, gathers speed north of Finsbury Park with the 16.05 to York on May 31st 1962. The Deltics had started intensive diagrams a few weeks before, and one would have been hauling the 'Talisman'. Unless it was late departing, I doubt the A4 would have been checked by the newcomer. Harringay's distants are off for the A4 and the 15.54 DMU on the slow. Tender: A4 corridor No.5592. (P J Groom)

SILVER FOX at speed at Essendine on June 9th 1957 with an up express. The tender is the original A4 corridor No.5592. It had been the first of the original engines to receive a Kylchap double blast, in May 1957. (The Transport Treasury)

The seldom (successfully) photographed SPARROW HAWK ambles through Princes St Gardens in May 1959, on its way to pick up its train from Waverley. With the start of the 'Talisman' Gateshead's A4s were given a long-overdue clean, and ran well. Whether recruitment was difficult or budget provision simply did not exist, Gateshead was a byword for dirty locomotives. It seemed to be accepted that their mechanical condition was fine, but certainly the effort needed to keep their Pacifics clean as well seemed to overwhelm the depot all too often. Tender: A4 non-corridor No.5668. (D H Beecroft, The Transport Treasury) *Inset.* The nameplate of the most elusive A4 – SPARROW HAWK. (R F Orpwood, Gresley Society Trust)

A magnificent photograph of SPARROW HAWK, in pre-war finery, roaring through the old Hadley Wood station with the 'Flying Scotsman'. The period must be 1938/39 when Gateshead had a share in the working on the '10 o'clock'. It looks as though it has been strengthened with an extra leading coach. The tender is A4 non-corridor No.5668. (Gresley Society Trust)

BITTERN hauling an RCTS special between Leeds and Glasgow over the Settle-Carlisle line. She is now in private ownership. The train is just north of Rise Hill Tunnel, July 16th 1967. Tender: A4 non-corridor No.5638. (M Mensing)

Left. BITTERN, now a Ferryhill A4, pulls away from Coupar Angus on April 16th 1965. Quite what the slogan on the boiler cladding means, I cannot say. Answers once again on a postcard to the Irwell Press. Tender: A4 non-corridor No.5638. (The Transport Treasury)

Below. BITTERN, in splendid external condition, rolls into Waverley through Princes St Gardens on the up Glasgow line. That does not mean that it was a Glasgow train since there were crossovers farther out, enabling Aberdeen coaches to cross to platform 10, for example. An inter-Regional express hauled by a 'Peak' Type 4 diesel passes on the down Glasgow, November 15th 1964. Tender: A4 non-corridor No.5638. (The Transport Treasury)

GUILLEMOT at Gateshead on June 5th 1948, resplendent in garter blue livery. She has been kept clean since overhaul 7-8 months ago, too, by the look of the tell-tale lines of bolts and boiler bands. The A4 has her usual tender, A4 non-corridor No.5669. (W G Boyden, courtesy Frank Hornby)

GUILLEMOT more as I remember her, sadly, dirty and an unusual visitor down south. She is passing Doncaster in 1953 with what looks like the 10.5 Kings Cross-Glasgow, which means that she came on at Peterborough, a Gateshead duty. Her tender is A4 non-corridor No.5669. (G W Goslin, Gresley Society Trust)

GUILLEMOT begins the descent of Cockburnspath bank at Penmanshiel, May 31st 1952. Just to prove that there are exceptions to every rule, for once she is nicely cleaned, despite not having a general overhaul between April 1950 and April 1953. The condition of the paintwork indicates an intermediate repaint, in November 1951, but however well she had been cleaned, it would not eliminate the ingrained dirt round the boiler bands for example. Tender: A4 non-corridor No.5669. (W Hermiston, The Transport Treasury).

WILD SWAN with an up express at Barnby Moor & Sutton, north of Retford. The occasion must be between early 1938 and autumn 1939. The A4 has her original non-corridor tender, No.5671. (The Transport Treasury)

WILD SWAN at Kings Cross with sister A4 LORD FARINGDON, with Copley Hill's A1 KITTIWAKE in March 1962. The A4 tenders were A4 and A3 corridors Nos.5651 and 5325 respectively. (T Wright)

Doncaster's new acquisition in 1938, MALLARD climbs the bank to Stoke south of Grantham. She has an almost clear chimney despite the undoubted effort with her heavy train. (Cawston Bequest, Canon Brian C. Bailey Collection)

MALLARD with the southbound 'Anglo-Scottish Car Carrier' at North Muskham in June 1960. Bathley Lane signalbox is in the distance, while closer to the camera the buildings either side of the line have an obvious air of 'railway' about them. The overbridge has probably been rebuilt more recently, but I would guess that, originally, the railway was crossed on the level, and these were the buildings associated with that level crossing. Possibly there was once also a goods depot and a siding or two. The A4 is coasting towards the troughs to the south. Tender: A3 corridor No.5330. (D H Beecroft, The Transport Treasury)

By Appointment! MALLARD's cab is the location for a Royal inspection. I don't think A4s normally carried notices such as 'Mind your head', although many places, especially the corridor tender, certainly needed one. This is the Marylebone Exhibition of rolling stock 11-14th May 1961, held to mark the Golden Jubilee of the Institution of Locomotive Engineers.

The Northern Rubber Special, 1X08, on September 30th 1961, with a glistening MALLARD, sailing along with little effort. The photo was taken somewhere to the north of Doncaster en route for Blackpool. The tender is A3 corridor No.5330. (B K B Green, Initial Photographics)

GOLDEN EAGLE, just out of Doncaster Plant, at the head of a down express at Grantham in June 1960. Tender: A4 non-corridor No.5667. (D H Beecroft, The Transport Treasury)

GOLDEN EAGLE sails through Ganwick with the Non-stop in the summer of 1937. The A4 only had a corridor tender, A3 corridor tender No.5323 seen here, for five years. (Cawston Bequest, Canon Brian C Bailey Collection)

The 10.5 Kings Cross-Glasgow was known pre-war as the 'Junior Scotsman' and was usually hauled, in the summer, by the Haymarket A4 held in reserve for the Non-stop. On August 4th 1951 the A4 was KINGFISHER, seen here at Warkworth. She has her original A3 corridor tender No.5331. (Cawston Bequest, Canon Brian C Bailey Collection)

The sight of an A4 and N2 pre-war would almost certainly suggest Kings Cross, but on this occasion it was Eastfield, which had its own N2s as well as visiting A4s such as KINGFISHER from Haymarket. The date is June 26th, 1938, and the tender is A3 corridor No.5331. (R J Buckley, Initial Photographics)

KINGFISHER in the summer of 1966, pounding up the hard climb out of Aberdeen at Cove Bay with the 17.30 Glasgow express. The A4s ran well on these trains, but with faltering maintenance and the lure of a comfortable chair in a diesel locomotive, their days were numbered. Three months later this, the last A4, was withdrawn for scrap. The tender is A3 corridor No.5329. (P J Coster)

KINGFISHER was one of the less frequent visitors to the southern end of the East Coast route on the 'Elizabethan' for no better reason than her general overhauls were less fortuitously timed than some of her Scottish sisters. A capable engine, regularly manned by two drivers named McLeod (but unrelated) KINGFISHER was often the reserve engine rather than the principal. The date is August 7th 1961, and the location is north of Sandy. The tender is A3 type corridor No.5329. (The Transport Treasury)

KINGFISHER on August 26th 1966 with a Glasgow express. I do not recognise the location from this angle, but it is a Caledonian Railway station and not North British. Stonehaven seems the most likely from my limited experience of the route. Tender: A4 non-corridor No.5640. (A G Forsyth, Initial Photographics)

Left. The last A4, KINGFISHER, on the turntable at St Margarets depot, one week before she was condemned. (N Preedy)

Below. One of my favourite vantage points was Well Lane overbridge just by Hitchin South Signalbox. It was a remarkable structure for what was effectively a footpath, a single arch bridge leaping over four tracks, probably about 60ft span. It is now replaced, but the photograph was taken just beneath. FALCON is on an up express, whilst the down express is hauled by SILVER FOX, distinguished by the familiar fox on her boiler side. Her driver will be none too happy, since the distant is 'on', showing that something is crossing at Cambridge Junction or, less likely, the A4 has caught up with the preceding train. It is hard to date, and I cannot find anything that defines it closer than 1953-1957 apart from two months in the summer of 1955 when her A3 corridor tender No.5330 was temporarily replaced by an A4 version. (Transport Treasury)

FALCON arrives, and then backs her freight, from Newcastle, into Millerhill Yard, south-east of Edinburgh. It is later than 1961, probably 1963 when she had gone to New England. It was certainly sad to see fine express locomotives reduced to filthy hulks on freight turns.

The non-stop 'Flying Scotsman' passes through Ganwick behind KESTREL in the summer of 1937. KESTREL, later renamed MILES BEEVOR, was at Haymarket at the time, although for most of her existence she was a southern engine. As with other A4s Miles Beevor, however admirable a fellow, could never rival, in the naming stakes, our most familiar falcon. Now Windhover, the country usage for Kestrel, would have been a good name... The tender was A3 corridor tender No.5324. (Cawston Bequest, Canon Brian C Bailey Collection)

An unusual shot of the down 'West Riding'. Apart from the first six months when re-introduced post-war, this train was almost always worked in both directions by a Copley Hill engine and men, mainly a Peppercorn A1 but sometimes one of their A3s. I would say that the number of occasions when an A4 was turned out for the down service were very few indeed. There is little doubt about the train, for it has the articulated twin sets off the pre-war 'West Riding Limited'. Dating is tricky: the engine is carrying a 34A shed plate, it is dark blue, and it has an A3 corridor tender. This places it firmly between September 1951 and October 1952 when the tender was changed. The A4 was supposed to have been fitted with experimental ATC in October 1950, but there is no evidence of its presence. Either the ATC was removed or the date for the fitting is wrong. The long guard irons are in place, which confirms summer 1952. The location is just north of the old Stevenage station, in the cutting leading down to Wymondley. The tender is A3 corridor No.5329. (The Transport Treasury)

A shabby MILES BEEVOR flanked by two interlopers, CREPELLO and a sister Deltic, at Kings Cross. The period is probably 1962, and the tender is A4 non-corridor No.5642. (Transport Treasury)

An A4 in the afterlife, on August 3rd 1966 at Perth. MILES BEEVOR had been withdrawn nearly eight months previously, but was sent to Crewe with SIR NIGEL GRESLEY to contribute to the latter's preservation, principally the coupled wheels I remember. A somewhat academic point (mentioned elsewhere) was that the two A4s were coupled to the tenders that first achieved 100mph officially (A3 corridor No.5324) and 126mph (The original A4 non-corridor No.5642, then cut up.)

MERLIN, on July 5th 1951, waits to leave Kings Cross with 'Capitals Limited'. She is BR blue, and much of her train was still in teak livery. Her fireman having seen the A4 coupled, is looking round. She has her usual A4 corridor tender, No.5652. (J F Aylard)

The 'Elizabethan' sets off from Waverley in 1960 behind Haymarket's most prolific A4, MERLIN. This unusual angle comes the footpath up to the former Calton Jail, known locally as 'Jacob's Ladder'. The photographer needed not only to be proficient but fit as well! A4 corridor No.5652. (P Wilson, G R Whitelaw Collection)

The stars of 1959! Haymarket's MERLIN coasts past Crescent Junction with the down 'Elizabethan', 1958-60; this and WALTER K. WHIGHAM below made 115 trips on the Non-stop between them in 1959. Of these MERLIN did sixty-two. The tender is A4 corridor No.5652. (B Richardson, The Transport Treasury)

WALTER K WHIGHAM at Kings Cross on September 9th 1959, with a sister standing behind. The engine is being prepared for another trip on the Non-stop; it made 53 journeys in 1959, by far the best Top Shed performance. Notice the Flaman drive bracket still in position, some two decades after the recorders were regularly used. I have the strong impression that liaison between the works and the drawing office was somewhat tenuous post-war, and locomotives were reassembled at Doncaster unquestioningly, unless a works order required an alteration. Tender: A4 corridor No.5649. (R F Smith, The Transport Treasury)

WALTER K WHIGHAM starts off confidently with the Royal Train on June 8th 1961. The crew's confidence was not shared by the photographer when a cross-London freight lumbered into York Road platform as the A4 moved. However, the guardian angel of photographers provided a stop signal to hold the freight, and an International Harvester tractor afforded a gap just large enough to record the magnificent sight. (P J Coster)

Below. Although the notes on the reverse give the date as June 29th 1955, this shot is seven years older, for only in 1948-49 was WOODCOCK attired in the mercifully short-lived purple livery. She is hauling the down non-stop 'Flying Scotsman' on Holloway Bank in July-August 1948. In fact, it could even have been one of the occasions when the Non-stop run was 408.65 miles, via Kelso and St Boswells on the Waverley route. Who knows? The train is composed of post-war LNER steel bodied stock, referred to as 'Thompson', although on introduction it was called 'Newton' stock. Despite being somewhat illogically clad in teak printed rexine, the stock looked splendid, and rode superbly at all speeds. The headboard is the old plate version which was superseded by the cast aluminium a year or so later. The driver appears to have closed the regulator for some reason which will not have gone down well on the footplate with so far to go! The location is just north of Holloway bank, with the top of the bank at Holloway North Down signalbox near the rear of the train. Tender: A4 corridor No.5648.

WOODCOCK waits at Kings Cross with a down express while a nicely cleaned N2 0-6-2T, No.69541, waits with her empty train before pounding out to Holloway Carriage Sidings. The date is mid-1958, and the tender is A3 corridor No.5323. (P J Coster)

WOODCOCK heads the down 4.21pm semi-fast north of New Southgate on 22 April 1963, in the last few days when there were cleaners at Top Shed. Tender No.5323. (Canon Brian C Bailey)

GOLDEN FLEECE gathers speed through Low Fell with the southbound 'Flying Scotsman' on a dull day in 1938-39. Tender: A4 corridor No.5650. (The Transport Treasury)

The up 'Elizabethan' emerges from Hadley Wood South Tunnel on 29th June 1954 behind GOLDEN FLEECE. The leading BG has been painted to a different specification to the rest of the train, and looks odd. The tender is A3 corridor No.5327. (Cawston Bequest, Canon Brian C Bailey Collection)

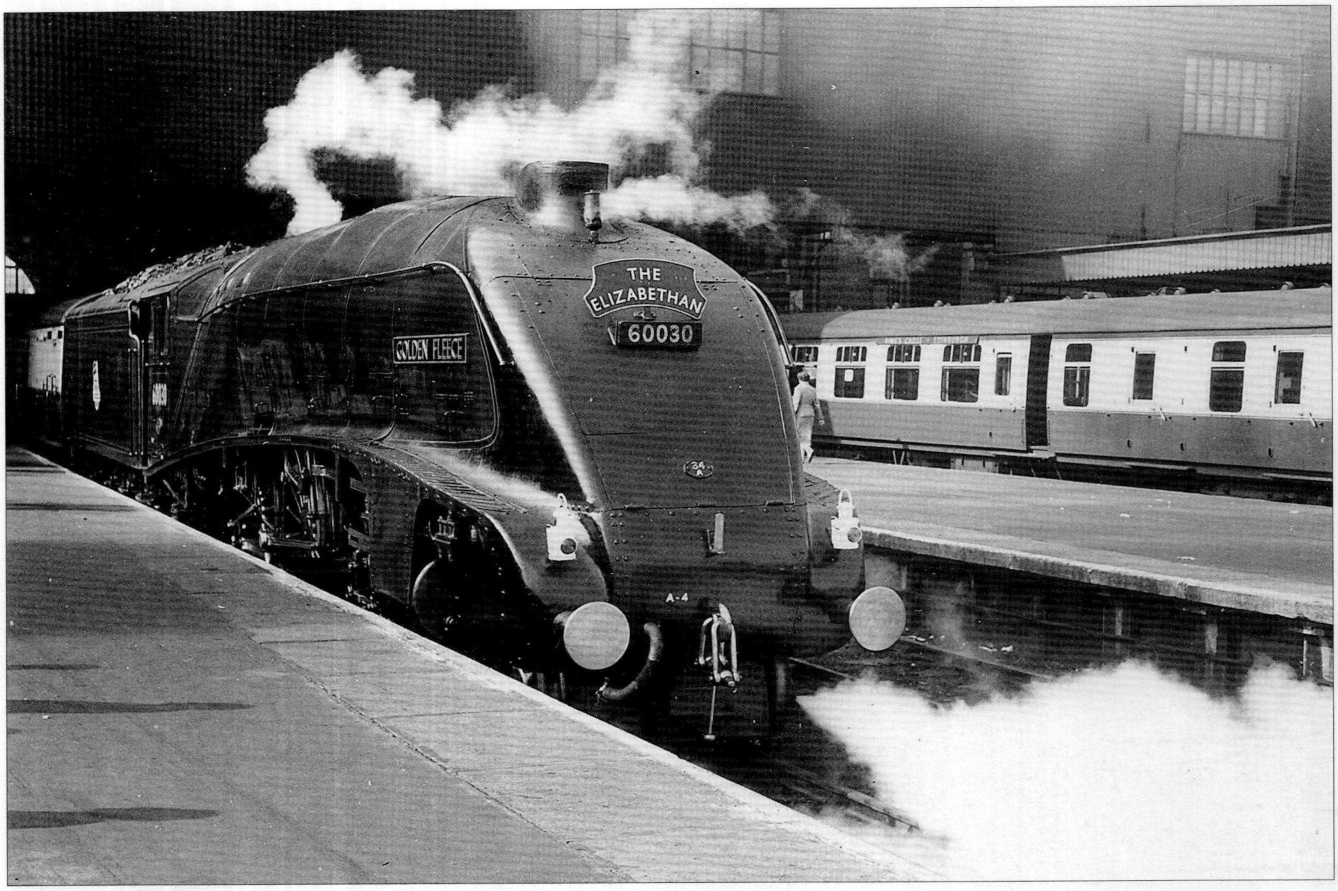

GOLDEN FLEECE buffers up to the 'Elizabethan' in platform 6 at Kings Cross. I think it is summer 1954, and it may well be the first Non-stop of the year. That year Kings Cross prepared two A4s hitherto unused on the Non-stop post-war, GOLDEN FLEECE and GANNET, and both ran well. Tender: A3 corridor No.5327.

GOLDEN PLOVER stands in old Platform 6 at Kings Cross with the Elizabethan in the summer of 1958 or later. The A4 now has a double chimney and is carrying the Scottish Region headboard; the nameplate and headboard have the Regional pale blue as a background colour. The tender is A4 corridor No.5650. (The Transport Treasury)

GANNET in garter blue livery, with the 16.00 from Kings Cross at Potters Bar on April 22nd 1948. The train barely seems to merit a splendid locomotive, especially with a short wheelbase vehicle at the front. Vintage coaching stock might be a joy to behold but only for others to travel in. The tender is A4 non-corridor No.5675. (Cawston Bequest, Canon Brian C Bailey Collection)

GANNET at New England, having arrived off the 'Heart of Midlothian'. The period must be 1959-60, the tender A3 corridor No.5331. (B. Richardson, The Transport Treasury)

GANNET heads north at New Southgate with an evening Leeds service in the last few months of steam traction. The crew have taken a good load of coal on board, by the look of the tender. The tender is A3 corridor No.5331. (P J Coster)

No details are given, but clearly this is 1938-39, almost certainly at Gateshead. SEAGULL was a popular choice for the streamliners and the heavier duties of the day. At the time she had an A4 non-corridor tender No.5636. (Transport Treasury)

The most frequent and successful performers on the post-war Non-stop, by short heads, were SEAGULL, UNION OF SOUTH AFRICA and MERLIN. Here we see SEAGULL pulling away from platform 10 at Waverley with one of the last 'Capitals Limited' services, on September 13th 1952. The A4 was, as always, magnificently clean. Tender: A3 corridor No.5325. (W Hermiston, The Transport Treasury)

A down Newcastle express waits at Grantham behind LORD FARINGDON in August 1960. Tender: A3 corridor No.5325. (D H Beecroft, The Transport Treasury)

The last A4, PEREGRINE, on the Top Shed turntable in 1939, some ten years before being renamed after the Lord Faringdon. The fireman has connected the brake pipe to the vacuum tractor which operated the turntable. She had A4 non-corridor tender No.5639, but that was exchanged for No.5642 within the year.

Bill Hoole brings an immaculate LORD FARINGDON on the 'Flying Scotsman' steadily through Peterborough North on July 27th 1957. Bill and Brian Bailey exchange greetings. The tender is A3 corridor No.5325. (P J Coster)

One of the two beavertail observation cars, E1729E, on Basingstoke turntable. The beavertails were rarely used on the main line for which they were built, but Alan Pegler managed to include them in several of his famous Northern Rubber Specials. On September 12th 1954, the first large Ivatt Atlantic, GNR No.251, assisted by 'Director' No.62663 PRINCE ALBERT, took the train far away into malachite green territory at Basingstoke, where the photo was taken. (L Elsey)

The first SIR RALPH WEDGWOOD rolls an up express through Alnmouth on August 11th 1939, three weeks before the outbreak of war. The Gateshead A4 has her original non-corridor tender No.5672. (R J Buckley, Initial Photographics)

The newly rebuilt W1, No.10000, passes the site of Ganwick signalbox with a down Newcastle express. The W1 is going easily, and has her A3 type corridor tender No.5484.

The new high pressure compound, probably outside Darlington Works, mated with her tender, A3 corridor No.5484. The fact that the locomotive and tender were designed by different people 76 miles apart must have been painfully obvious when the two were coupled, since the profiles of the rakish cab and A3 corridor tender parted company above footplate level – if they even met there! The conjunction of the rear axle with its Cortazzi self-centring axleboxes, and the Bissel truck behind must have exercised the design team. (Transport Treasury)

No.60700 at Kings Cross on Friday August 5th 1955. The curiously long cab and rear axles are well depicted. It seems inexplicable that BR did not authorise works to rebuild such singletons as GREAT NORTHERN and the W1 to the standard design and avoid the problems of uniqueness, rather than concentrate on their own often second rate designs. I have a record of most of the day's operation, but there is no mention of the W1. From the angle of the sun I think it must be an early evening Hull express between 18 and 19.00 for which I have no notes. Even amateur signalmen needed a meal! The W1 is in good external condition, and the road is set for Main 1, while an outer suburban train is set for Main 2. A4 non-corridor tender No.5639. (B K B Green, Initial Photographics)

Doncaster's No.60700 gathers speed effortlessly through Hornsey with the 16.05 Leeds and York express on August 24th 1958. An inner suburban train on the up slow has the BR compartment stock that gradually replaced the famous LNER quad-art stock. A4 non-corridor tender No.5639. (Peter Groom)

THE BLACK BOX... THE BLACK BOX...

THERE'S MORE!

Though blessed with a decent memory and many years travelling over the East Coast main line, there are times when a photograph, with no overleaf clues to help, stares blankly and accusingly back off my desk, and no spark of recognition is struck. Resort to an arsenal of documents, books and magazines usually unearths the answer but there are the hard cases. Then I have to type the words that say 'I pass'. People have been most kind and helpful, and with enlightenment comes the feeling 'of course, how could I have been so blind?' Over to Irwell Press...

***

Regretfully errors creep in to these volumes; very rarely (it is a relief to report) do they concern the locomotive details but rather they are idiotic typographical slip-ups which seem impossible to completely hunt down and destroy, calamities such as the wrong image selected at the last minute by a publisher desiring good but failing. Take pages 59 and 60 in *A4 Accompaniment:1*. The lower picture page 59 should swap places with the upper picture page 60.

But enough of that! Canon Brian Bailey, who haunted the GN with Peter Coster for many years, writes: 'Unlike Peter I am not an engineer, but a historian and sociologist as well as a theologian and so my concerns for accuracy come from a different angle from Peter's, hence we can complement one another, apart from having known each other since we were 14! First, the captions in *A4 Accompaniment:2*. On page 44 and 45, there are photos of 60028 and 60029. The one of '28' was taken in June/July 1948 as it shows one of early runs of the down 1 p.m. Kings Cross to Edinburgh, when equipped with the plum and spilt milk experimental livery. This train and the North Briton were the two East Coast line trains chosen for this experiment, and at the start they had nominated engines which were also painted in the first purple blue style. The A4s chosen were 60024 and 60027 at Haymarket and 60028 and 60029 at Kings Cross. In 1951 the mid-day train to Edinburgh was retimed to 2 p.m. completely re-equipped with the first Mark 1 BR standard coaches and named the Heart of Midlothian. The other caption on page 45 is of 60029 on the *down* Non-stop in summer 1960, approaching Edinburgh. The two clues, despite the smoke, are the Edinburgh suburban skyline and the junction the train is crossing. This is the connection coming from the Waverley route from Carlisle just before Portobello. This and several other photos of the Non-stop near the end of their journeys reveal how economic in coal the double blast A4s were on this working'.

Others confirm the solution as Portobello East. Dr Hugh Morton writes: 'I am pretty sure that the location on page 45 in *A4 Accompaniment:2* is Portobello East Junction, a few miles east of Waverley, and that the Non-stop in on its very last lap into Edinburgh'. Mr Stephen Turnbull also writes: 'I can confirm this is Portobello East Junction. The A4 is on the down Elizabethan (due in Waverley around 4.05pm) and is crossing the junction where the Waverley Route joins the East Coast main line. The sidings in the background are part of Portobello yards. The embankment, also in the background is the single line known as the Lothians Line which provided an avoiding line for goods traffic coming up from the Leith docks and goods yard area to Niddrie yards and the East Coast main line at Newhailes Junction. The photograph has probably been taken from the pedestrian overbridge which used to run across the lines beside the Portobello East signal box'.

Dr Morton again: 'From 1961 to 1967 I pursued my medical undergraduate studies at Dundee. The arrival of a fresh batch of A4s in Scotland was a major event, and I enjoyed some fine runs on the Glasgow-Aberdeen trains, when I should have been at my books. Moreover, towards the end of the A4s it was possible to get an unofficial and highly irregular footplate trip, by taking the 23.00 from Glasgow to Perth on a Saturday night; or even on a weeknight, when the train conveyed a sleeper for Inverness. At Glasgow, there was a furtive lookout for the attention of the footplate crew – and it was at times necessary to form an orderly queue, such was the demand. The first man would ride out to Cumbernauld; there he would be replaced by number two in the queue, to Larbert. Although the footplate crew took care to avoid the attentions of the Inspector at Stirling, the stop at Gleneagles made for a 'third leg' of the rota before Perth! Thus it was that, on a cold winter evening, I had the huge satisfaction of sampling, albeit in a small way, what it was like to ride on one of Gresley's, and the world's, finest locomotives'.

In *A4 Accompaniment:1* on page 13 Britannia 70039 SIR CHRISTOPHER WREN was inexplicably titled HEREWARD THE WAKE (thanks to Mr Frank Cook for pointing out this lapse). On a brighter note, Mr Irving Nicol offers the following expansionary comments: 'Firstly *A4 Accompaniment:1*. On page 20 4489 on the Haymarket table would have worked the down Flying Scotsman from Kings Cross; this is an evening photograph with the sun on the other side. The photograph on page 22 of 60011 is of interest for it was taken on the first day of operation of the 3 hour service, 18 June 1962, on the 7.10am Aberdeen-Glasgow. The driver certainly is whistling, as noted, but is doing so because the train was running late. The Power Box at Perth had signalled the train into the wrong platform which had no water column. The A4 then had to be run forward and reversed back into the station to take water, repeating it all to couple back on to its train. The 7.10 left Perth 20 minutes late that morning. No doubt there were a few telephone calls but it arrived in Buchanan Street only 12 minutes late, not bad for a first day. On page 30 60016 is working the 3.30pm Aberdeen Postal, and will work the Postal portion of the train through to Carstairs, returning from Carstairs the following morning with the northbound Postal for Aberdeen. On page 36 60019 is standing at the south end of Perth station, almost certainly in 1966, with the 5.15pm Aberdeen-Glasgow 3 hour express.

'In *A4 Accompaniment:2,* on page 21 60012 is standing on the disposal pits at Dundee Tay Bridge shed, as suggested. On page 27 60016 is just south of Aberdeen station approaching Ferryhill Junction. On page 35, yes QUICKSILVER was the standby loco for the Aberdeen Flyer from Edinburgh to Aberdeen. On the day before, Friday, 60015 had worked the 4pm Talisman from Kings Cross through to Edinburgh to be ready on Haymarket shed that Saturday morning. I tried to get the Running Foreman, Bob Greig, to roster 60015 on the 4.30pm Edinburgh-Perth and return that same Saturday, but no – what a pity. MERLIN on page 42 is on the booked St Rollox A4 turn, the 5.15pm Aberdeen-Glasgow.'

Irving Nicol's comments are interesting writes Peter Coster. *One point: QUICKSILVER did not work down on May 25th 1962 from Kings Cross on the 'Talisman' but from Newcastle. She headed the 11.00 from Kings Cross earlier in the day. I was on the train, and it was a poor run. No doubt the driver had been looking forward to one of Gateshead's Deltics and was not pleased with a trip down memory lane.*